BACCHUS

1973
GOES TO THE
Movies

BACCHUS

by

MYRON TASSIN

With an Introduction to Mardi Gras by

FRANCES PARKINSON KEYES

PELICAN PUBLISHING COMPANY

GRETNA 1975

ISBN: 088289–061–1

PHOTO CREDITS

Jane Boulen: pages 88, 89; *Dixie Roto:* 68 (bottom), 69; Christopher R. Harris: 72, 78, 80-83, 86; Blaine Kern Collection: 55; Ronald LeBoeuf: 92; Louisiana Tourist Development Commission: 16, 17 (top); Giles Mateu: 24, 39, 40 (top left), 41 (bottom), 46, 47, 50, 52-54, 65, 67, 84; Z. J. Montz: 31-34, 51; New Orleans Tourist and Convention Commission: 13, 14, 18, 19; Sonny Randon Studio: 41 (top), 49, 56-64, 77, 85; Ralph Romaguera: 87, 90, 93; Angela Shelley: 17 (bottom left and right), 68 (top); *Times-Picayune* staff: 40 (top right), 43, 45.

Library of Congress Cataloging in Publication Data

Tassin, Myron.
Bacchus.
1. New Orleans—Carnival. I. Title.
GT4211.N4T37 394.2'5'0922 74–20526

Designed by Barney McKee
Manufactured in the United States of America
Published by Pelican Publishing Company, Inc.
630 Burmaster Street, Gretna, Louisiana 70053

To my wife and best friend, Shirley

Contents

For their assistance and support, most grateful acknowledgments to:

AUGUST PEREZ, III

OWEN E. BRENNAN, JR.

RICHARD BRENNAN

BLAINE KERN

For arranging clearance to use Frances Parkinson Keyes' "An Introduction to Mardi Gras," thanks to:

BONNIE NIXON,
The Greater New Orleans
Tourist & Convention Commission

12
ZULU

An Introduction to Mardi Gras

by
FRANCES PARKINSON KEYES

In the year of Grace 1872, the Mardi Gras crowds which thronged Canal Street in New Orleans suddenly appeared "to go wild." For hours they had been patiently awaiting the arrival of a gorgeous procession. But even before Rex, The King of Carnival, clad in purple velvet and riding on a bay charger, made his spectacular appearance, the music which heralded his approach filled the air with lilting melody. By the time a milk-white ox—the "Boeuf Gras" of fond tradition—came stepping along, wreathed in ribbons and garlanded with flowers, everyone was singing, or trying to sing, a new song:

If Ever I Cease To Love,
If Ever I Cease To Love,
May The Fish Get Legs,
And The Cows Lay Eggs,
If Ever I Cease To Love.

The words were ridiculous, but the tune was irresistible. Besides, there was a thrilling and romantic story behind the new song. And if there is anything on earth which Orleanians love better than Carnival itself, this is a thrilling romance which, as a matter-of-fact, Carnival usually provides without much exterior help.

In this particular instance, cooperation had come from an unexpected quarter: A brother to the Czar of all the Russians, the Grand Duke Alexis, who was making a tour of the United States, had decided to include New Orleans in his itinerary because a fascinating actress, Lydia Thompson, was about to do the same.

Miss Thompson was currently appearing in a musical comedy, and she had charmed the Grand Duke with her singing in other cities. The theme song of her production was entitled, "If Ever I Cease To Love," and though the Grand Duke had not been conspicuous for the durability of his affections, there could be no question that, at the moment, these were vehemently involved.

The illustrious visitor had chartered the "floating palace," James Howard, for his visit, and it had reached the outskirts of New Orleans on the eve of Mardi Gras. As Perry Young, author of "The Mistick Krewe," put it:

> The holiday dawned beautiful and maskers were soon in the streets . . . the decorations of the business houses and of many residences . . . were profuse, with Rex' colors predominating—purple, gold and green, as then established by edict and accepted over since for Carnival.
>
> Galleries at all principal points were reserved exclusively for ladies . . . the parade was over a mile long . . . divided into five sections . . . the maskers remained on Canal Street, dancing and parading until dark to mingle, then unmask with the throngs who packed the streets to see the night procession of the Mistick Krewe.
>
> The Grand Duke, after viewing the torchlight pageant, entered the Comus Ball and was ushered into a box which had been reserved and decorated for him . . . he had occasioned the first Rex Parade and inspired the immortal Grand March of the Carnival . . . "If Ever I Cease To Love."

It is not known whether the outcome of his suit of Miss Thompson was equally successful.

This imperial visit, without question, should head the list of those which have made Mardi Gras outstanding. But from the earliest days of the French settlement there were Carnival celebrations of one sort or another, and the balls, banquets, and masquerades became more and more elaborate as the colony grew in size and wealth.

Traditionally, in France and Louisiana, Carnival lasts from Twelfth Night—the Sixth of January—to midnight of Mardi Gras, the day before Ash Wednesday.

Mardi Gras (literally translated, it means Fat Tuesday) is the traditional day of feasting before the beginning of Lent. Nothing could be more irritating to the average Louisianian than the vague assumption on the part of outsiders that Carnival and Mardi Gras are identical.

Many years after the ardors of the Czar's brother had become only a nostalgic memory, another royal visit, that of the Duke and Duchess of Windsor, in 1950, inspired Orleanians with an enthusiasm comparable to that aroused by the Grand Duke Alexis. Carnival royalty succumbed to the irresistible spell of the lovely lady for whom a real king had willingly renounced a throne. For days after the ducal couple had come and gone, the city rang with praises of her poise, her graciousness, and, above all, her perfect compliance with Carnival customs.

I should have been surprised if she had failed to reveal such attributes. Every woman in her family whom I have known—and I have known several of them well over a long period of years—is the happy possessor of style, wit, charm, and distinction. Nevertheless, this second ducal visit was marked by one small tempest in a teapot.

It so happens that it was a cousin of the Duchess who taught me to make the mint juleps which have since become one of my own specialties—and I had received a telegram from the Duchess saying that she and the Duke

Floats get final touchup.

would be glad to attend a small mint julep party at Beauregard House before the dinner at Antoine's and the Carnival ball to which they were afterward going.

I was at Crowley, in the heart of the rice district, nearly 200 miles from New Orleans when this welcome news reached me and I immediately sent out invitations. These were hardly in the mail when I received a telephone call from Mr. Dermot Mac Dermot, the British Consul General.

"As you probably know, the Duke and Duchess were in Mexico on a hunting trip, when they decided to include New Orleans in their return itinerary to New York," he reminded me. ("How history repeats itself," I said to myself. "The Grand Duke Alexis also made his decision to attend Carnival on the spur of the moment.") "The Duke naturally did not include full dress in his equipment for such an expedition," Mr. Mac Dermot continued. "I must therefore ask you to request all your male guests to wear black ties and dinner coats instead of white ties and tails to your party."

HOLSUM
CAFETERIA
HOTEL
TECHE
HOTEL

I said I would comply with his request and put in a series of long distance calls. In almost every case, I was able to reach a prospective guest without much loss of time. But there was one with whom I was unable to make prompt connections. I sent him a note by special delivery and—somewhat tardily because of the delay caused by much telephoning—set out for New Orleans to begin preparations for my party. These were almost immediately interrupted by a call from my elusive friend, who addressed me with severity.

"You will have to telephone everyone all over again," he commanded, "and tell them to wear white ties and tails after all. The Duke cannot come to our ball in a dinner jacket!"

Somewhat startled, I murmured that I did not feel it was proper for me to tell the Duke of Windsor what he ought to wear to a ball or on any other occasion.

"Very well," my friend retorted, still more severely. "Then I shall tell him myself."

He was as good as his word. The Windsors were traveling in the private car of Mr. Robert Young, president of the Chesapeake and Ohio Railroad, who had been their host during their Mexican hunting trip. When the train rolled into the station, my friend was waiting for it.

He delivered his ultimatum, and the Duke good naturedly wired New York. His distracted secretary, after something of a search, unearthed the requisite garments and sent them to New Orleans by air mail.

The Duke, like the Duchess, gave entire satisfaction at the Carnival ball which they attended.

Though the celebration of Carnival takes so joyous a form, the esteem in which it is held is one almost approaching reverence, and the preparations for it are made with a thoroughness and a gravity which the outsider finds hard to understand.

What is more, these preparations are all basically made by men, or—as the Louisianian would be careful to tell you—by gentlemen.

The official balls are all invitation affairs, given by male societies known as Krewes. Next to the error of supposing that Carnival and Mardi Gras are synonymous, the error of assuming that Carnival balls are public is the one most resented by Louisianians.

But though the gentlemen undoubtedly supply the power behind every Carnival throne, it is the lady chosen to grace it who revels in the white light which beats upon it. There is little exaggeration in the oft-repeated pleasantry that the first words voiced by the average New Orleans young mother, after learning that her newborn infant is a girl, is the fervent exclamation, "Oh, how I hope she will be a Carnival Queen some day!"

With this end in view, drastic economies are often made for years, and the girl who gives up the advantages of superior education, extended travel, and similar benefits usually does so willingly and even eagerly, for she shares her mother's hopes and is willing to make almost any sacrifice if there is a reasonable prospect that this will result in the coveted honor.

When the time draws near for her debut, she waits, not only breathlessly,

Nothing matches Mardi Gras for crowd appeal.

but prayerfully for the notification that she has been chosen to reign at one of the balls.

After the notification comes a series of conferences. Until the prospective Queen knows the theme of the tableau in which she is to appear and its color scheme, she cannot approach her dressmaker on the subject of a design for her royal robes, and these are the next important consideration.

When they are in readiness she has the added satisfaction of seeing the regalia, which is the gift of the Krewe over which she is to reign, displayed in a show window of the great Holmes Department Store—crown, sceptre, earrings, necklace, and bracelets in all their glittering splendor. And then comes the time when they are hers to wear!

A special police escort has been assigned to her and the maids in her court. Limousines are provided to take them to the Auditorium, and here a striped awning overhead and a strip of spotless canvas across the sidewalk proclaim that everything is in readiness for their reception.

Salute to Tennessee Williams.

The Grand March around the ballroom usually marks the first triumphal appearance within, before the King and Queen take their places on their thrones. Then the masked members of the Krewe giving the ball—and the ladies who are their chosen partners—approach the dais to make obeisance. After that, dancing becomes general. Each masker carries a sack over his arm and from this, at the end of every dance, he extracts a small package containing a gift and presents it to his partner.

There is always one "official" favor, but there are many others which are unofficial. Under the helpful cloak of anonymity, gifts of greater value than would otherwise be offered or accepted are occasionally bestowed. And who shall say that they should not be at such a time?

The queens of all the major Carnival balls enjoy the privilege of watching the great Mardi Gras parade from the balcony of the Boston Club, where it is reviewed by the Queen of Carnival. Down Canal Street it comes in all its glory with its bands playing, its floats moving majestically forward, and its maskers tossing glittering baubles to the waiting throng. For an hour or more the procession winds down the wide avenue, filling it with tuneful hilarity and transforming it to a scene of splendor. But the supreme moment of Carnival has not yet arrived.

This comes with the meeting of Rex and his Queen and Comus, another high dignitary of the festival, and his Queen, with their respective suites, in the presence of their joint Krewes and their selected guests. In the Grand March which brings the balls to an end, Comus and Rex exchange partners. And at the Queen's supper which follows these two final balls, which take place simultaneously on opposite sides of the Auditorium, the King of Carnival takes his place between the two Queens.

Then a final toast is drunk and the Carnival song is sung for the last time and the flags of purple and green and gold come down. Mardi Gras is over. Ash Wednesday has come.

This—in brief and in general—is what happens year after year in New Orleans. However, each Carnival season brings with it its own special welcome, its own special tempo, and its own special climax. And every now and then some distinguished visitor, or some episode, is outstanding—as

Costumed spectators eye crowd.

The unusual is commonplace at Mardi Gras.

Some faces look familiar.

A king greets his subjects.

in the case of the Grand Duke Alexis and the song which became the royal anthem.

Following his visit, the next especially noteworthy event occurred in 1884, when the daughters of four great Confederate leaders took part in the celebration of Carnival. Balls at that time were still held in the Old French Opera House, since then unfortunately destroyed by fire, and again, according to Perry Young's book "The Mistick Krewe":

> The entire Opera was occupied by ladies in the most brilliant costumes de bal.
>
> Gentlemen in their sober garb were no part of the prospect. They sat, if at all, in the rear and topmost spaces. The right-hand proscenium box was exquisitely decorated in garlands and wrought figures of flowers in honor of the special guests of Comus—the daughters of Robert E. Lee, Stonewall Jackson, Jefferson Davis and D. H. Hill.

The Misses Lee also attended a reception at the Washington Artillery, and their visit marked the unveiling of the Lee Statue. The latter ceremony had a

Royalty on parade.

touching sequel. Several days later, according to the Daily Picayune-Times Democrat of that time,

> [a] gallant and grizzly old soldier, armed with a basket of flowers . . . repaired to the mansion of Col. A. H. May. Sending in his card, he was met at the door by one of the ladies of the household, who told him the Misses Lee were just going out to spend the evening, and while not at home to other visitors would receive him with the greatest of pleasure, and ushered him into the drawing room.
>
> Soon after the ladies came in and Captain Blesel was presented and was graciously received. . . . The old soldier of the Union said he knew General Lee not as his own soldiers knew him but as a brave knows a brave, as honor salutes honor, as chivalry and soldierhood pay homage to the genius and nobility of a great commander. He had expressed the sentiments from the bottom of his heart. . . . Miss Mildred Lee said words failed to express her feelings on this occasion. . . . The entire affair made a profound impression on all parties present.

Almost every Carnival season is followed by an epidemic of engagements. "If Ever I Cease To Love" is appropriate both as a theme song and a royal anthem because it voices the feeling, not merely of those newly betrothed, but of rich and poor, young and old, sick and well—in fact, of practically the entire population of South Louisiana.

The major official balls are exclusive, but there is hardly a social organization or an educational institution which does not elect a queen and celebrate Carnival with due ceremony. When the general masking begins at dawn on Mardi Gras, "cook's son, duke's son, son of a hundred kings" are out on the streets together, while the Colonel's lady and Judy O'Grady are sisters not only under their skins, but in the merriment of their mood. When dusk comes, and with it the removal of masks, everyone is tired, but everyone is in love with life, quite aside from the very large numbers of persons who are in love with one another.

It has been this way for several hundred years already. It will probably be this way for several hundred years more at least. Indeed, in my opinion, it is quite as likely that fish will get legs and cows lay eggs as that Louisiana will cease to love its Carnival and its Mardi Gras.

CHAPTER ONE

Resurrection of a God

"Insolent." "Gauche." "Upstarts." "Molesters of tradition." "A travesty on customs."

Like thistle puffs in March, aristocratic epithets swirled about as thirteen undaunted young men met in Adelaide Brennan's home on Prytania in 1968. Their objective—to organize a new, different, something-for-everyone Carnival krewe.

Reared in the heady evangelism of Mardi Gras and social conscious New Orleans, the thirteen latter-day Bacchus apostles knew, chapter and verse, the Thou Shalt's and Shalt Not's of rigid Carnival religion . . . a religion which traditionally defers contentedly to the precepts of the status quo. But they recognized a definite need for a catalytic event to bolster what they considered a sagging public interest in Carnival, particularly in Carnival Sunday. Following evening after evening of pageantry, paradeless Sunday night became a let-down for residents and visitors keyed-up in mounting anticipation of Fat Tuesday's grand crescendo.

Then, too, the "closed" structure of krewe memberships, parades, and balls discouraged participation by potential visitors who had the resources to travel to the Crescent City and leave behind considerable green lagniappe. True, Carnival hall rentals, favors, throws, costumes, evening clothes, dinners, floats, banquets, food, liquor, and labor all account for a thriving stimulation of local business. In reality, however, this economic propellant to a great extent simply switches money from one local pocket to another.

By 1965, the hotel–motel–restaurant industry was beginning to experience a definite softening of interest in Carnival. "People became more discerning, critical, perceptive, questioning during the Sixties," Dick Brennan explains. "In their inquisitiveness, they grew tired of accepting the world as it was."

BACCHUS

Like costumed cyclone fences, the members-only balls were discouraging jet setters and easy-spending middle class bon vivants from coming to New Orleans. "Besides dollars," Owen Brennan, Jr. states, "their absence was denying New Orleans amplified entertainment impact."

"Ah, but we have colorful parades for them," disciples of an isolationist Mardi Gras proffered as they professed their belief in Carnival as a strictly local affair. Big deal. Macy's department store and the Rose, Orange, and Cotton Bowls all were presenting first rate extravaganzas live and on television. Free.

Disconcerting feedback continued: "I drop a thousand bucks in New Orleans during Carnival. Pretty fat ticket for two or three parades and a handful of trinkets."

Let's concede for a moment that Carnival should never become tourist bait. What about the young, vibrant newcomers to New Orleans who were flying off to Mexican holidays or skiing in Aspen "during the season" rather than suffer the near indignation of outcasts? What about them?

A major obstacle to a Sunday night parade had been the unavailability of the Municipal Auditorium for the traditional dance afterwards. But Rivergate was a possibility now, so perhaps the time was ripe. Maybe the Bacchus wine had come of age. Why "Bacchus"? Marshall Pearce, the krewe's first president (elected when he missed a meeting), relates how the name came about:

> At an early meeting, designer–charter member Larry Youngblood suggested the organization call itself, "The Merry Knights of Camelot." No one but Larry knows if he was serious or not, but his suggestion caught on like a wet bandaid.
>
> Blaine Kern pointed out that the name "Bacchus" had been used twenty years previous by Owen Brennan, Sr. The late restaurateur had persuaded Dr. Henry LaRocca in the late Forties to restage a couple of his Alla Krewe balls in the Old Lyons Center for the edification of visitors.
>
> When "Pip" Brennan confirmed that the name was already copyrighted, and available, Marshall Pearce said, "Let's pick it up." Everyone present agreed.

A name doth not a krewe make. Doubts were still very much in evidence. Could the apostles pull it off? Or were they naive fools thinking they could recast the well-set Carnival mold?

George Chapman said, "Young men think old men are fools, but old men *know* young men are fools." Only problem, George ole boy, is that sometimes young men don't know they're fools when they attempt to accomplish the impossible. And succeed.

Pascal scolded Montaigne for declaring that "custom ought to be followed simply because it is custom, and not because it is reasonable or just." The apostles of change applauded Pascal.

"Change *is* traditional," they reasoned with the unreasonableness and groggy logic of prospective Bacchants. "We fight to preserve the sanctity of the Vieux Carré while building contemporary skyscrapers across Canal. As we organize and lobby to keep the St. Charles streetcars creeping along like oblong tortoises, we cruise along our interstates at several times that speed. We preserve the good of the past and present, while progressing into the future." All agreed with the premise that sounded much like a high school graduating class motto.

They were an assorted lot these determined wine god worshipers: businessmen, professionals, artists, media executives, optimists, pessimists, one apparent clairvoyant, a summarizer, and a half passel of devil's advocates. The list read almost like a "Who's Who" in the young community: Owen (Pip) Brennan, Jr., Dick Brennan, August Perez, III, Blain Kern, Harold Spaid, Larry Youngblood, Pete Moss, Marshall Pearce, Doug Regan, Bob Sonfield, Jim Nassikas, Dr. Ted Dampeer, and Carl Smith, Jr.

Guidelines were hammered out. Bacchus would in no way be social—no court, maids, queens, dukes. No tableaux. There would be no attempt to infringe upon any aspect of the aristocratic structure of Mardi Gras. Bacchus would simply seek to become the Hadacol that would fortify this festival of festivals by making Carnival's Sunday night an evening to remember by New Orleanians and visitors alike, rather than the comedown it had become.

All energies would pour into staging, to the best of the krewe's abilities and resources, the finest, biggest, best parade with the largest and most imaginative animated floats in the history of Mardi Gras. The number of favors, beads, and doubloons tossed to the crowd would eclipse anything ever before witnessed. Tractors pulling floats would be concealed to further minimize reality and deepen the spell cast in the dizzy world of revelry.

Blaine Kern, float designer–builder extraordinaire, who organizes and executes over forty parades a year, enthusiastically accepted the mammoth challenge.

Instead of a grand ball, members and guests would ALL participate actively in a huge dinner-dance, a rendezvous. A big-name band would play. Like one giant serpentine, the Bacchus floats would enter Rivergate to backdrop the dinner-dance sans the customary tableau.

To obviate the steadfast isolationist attitude, god Bacchus would be a nationally known celebrity possessing humanitarian leanings—an outsider to be admired by the throng of well-wishers for his contributions to his fellowman.

Such a celebrity, it was concluded, would feel the pulse of the people, gain instant rapport with his subjects, and lend his status, flair, and renown to certain success—not to mention the national publicity.

National publicity? Why not? As potent and prominent as are krewes like Rex and Comus, they parade on Tuesday when the vast majority of people in the country either are at work or at school. Consequently, national media coverage is poor and the audience is minimal. Bacchus would frolic on Sunday when the newsweek is at its ebb and hungry for material . . . when Americans are in their peak of leisure time.

In Euripides' Greek tragedy "Bacchae," the congregation of the faithful raised itself to a state of hysteria by means of musical ritual and, at the culminating moment, tore into pieces and devoured, hot and bleeding, the animal in which they thought their god to be temporarily incarnate. In the Carnival myth, the congregation of the Bacchus faithful would be raised to

Prime movers in creating the Bacchus krewe.

the state of near hysteria not only with music, but also with splendor, imaginative themes and floats, not to overlook spirits from the vine as well as from hops, corn, barley, rice, and potatoes. And don't forget an avalanche of throws. Wild, riotous merrymaking would be followed by dancing, feasting, and celebration.

When god Bacchus was received hospitably by his worshipers, he returned the kindness with a gift from the grape. The resurrected Bacchus would do more. Much more.

The New Orleans thirteen agreed to meet a month later at the Royal Orleans—each one inviting about twenty friends who might be interested in hearing about the Bacchus concept. Some 350 showed up. Like true disciples, the makeup of those present mirrored closely the personalities and convictions of the original circle. Examples:

DEVIL'S ADVOCATE: "Can we realistically hope to attract a truly important personality without a track record to offer? Without the promise of success? Wouldn't he be gambling his reputation with something that might not make it?" (If only the advocate had been able to see the future.)

States-Item, 2-17-69: *"The young krewe of Bacchus spared neither physical nor monetary effort to make an early name for itself. Tradition took a beating from this imaginative krewe as an 'outsider' reigned as Bacchus I. The non-resident was famed comedian Danny Kaye."*

PESSIMIST: "Assuming we have a successful maiden flight, and we all agree that Bacchus I must be a big name, I doubt that we can expect to keep up the quality of kings."

States-Item, 2-7-70: *"The krewe of Bacchus procession will begin at 6:30 P.M. tomorrow with television star Raymond Burr reigning over the krewe's second annual parade of merriment."*

OPTIMIST: "Our strength will come from the people. We can and must present to them monarchs they will recognize and like and revere."

Times-Picayune, 2-22-71: *"Lining the streets, packed in thicker than ever, the crowd pounced on doubloons and reached for beads which were being thrown out at a record rate.*

"And the crowd was cheering too. Cheering for the parade's king, Jim Nabors. A contagious cry of 'Gomer, Hey Gomer' rose from young and old alike all along the procession as the celebrity waved almost continuously, pausing only to throw out doubloons."

DEVIL'S ADVOCATE: "You can expect unrelenting flak for choosing an out-of-town king. Besides, you can't expect the citizenry to shower adulation, year after year, upon Hollywood kings."

States-Item, 2-14-72: *"Bacchus, the god of wine and merriment, thundered into the French Quarter late last night, and trundled out of record crowds there well after midnight.*

"Maskers on the mammoth, kinetic, electric floats people have come to associate with Bacchus, shoveled tons of doubloons, beads and giddiness to the throngs. . . .

"The parade itself began with the usual pomp and libation as Phil Harris, known for the night as Bacchus IV, toasted and sang his way down St. Charles through the Quarter, and into the Rivergate convention center. The parade over, the Quarter remained blanketed with humanity . . . and New Orleans went to bed wondering what was going to happen at this rate, come Mardi Gras."

CLAIRVOYANT: Looking up at the ceiling, fingertips massaging a large, balding forehead as if to conjure up hazy images, "I can see the day when Bacchus Sunday will strongly complement Fat Tuesday," and clearing his throat with his best Major Hoople harrumpf, continued, "when millions of Americans will know of our Krewe, will marvel at the spectacle."

New Orleans Magazine, 2-73: *"Bob Hope has some idea of what it's like, and to record it, he'll be making a television special out of his experience reigning as Bacchus and will share it with the whole country later on N.B.C."* (Would you believe 50 million viewers on March 7?)

SUMMARIZER: (Who apparently studied under the Clairvoyant), "Bacchus must be so successful that a former king may even wish to return to participate in a later carnival."

States-Item, 2-25-74: *"As it has been for several years, the high point of Carnival Sunday was the procession of Bacchus, who drew huge crowds all along his route despite a biting wind.*

"Country-pop singer Glen Campbell reigned as Bacchus VI. Riding a preceding float were former Bacchus kings Phil Harris and Jim Nabors. On the back of that float was a surprise participant, baseball great, Yogi Berra.

"As one parade watcher put it, 'it has to be some parade when they can put Yogi Berra on the back *of a float.' "*

By the time the organizational meeting at the Royal Orleans adjourned, some 270 people had committed themselves to membership.

About Bacchus' influence. The krewe helped put Rivergate on the map. Since its advent, other krewes have enlarged and improved their parades. Celebrity participants are being invited as a matter of course—in 1974, for example, the Queen of Endymion, Judy Behler, had Doc Severinson, television's Tonight Show orchestra leader, as her grand duke. Big bands are playing at several balls.

Carnival and Mardi Gras are generating more and better publicity for New Orleans. People around the country now know that the Crescent City not only has had no real race problem up to this point, but it is probably the only big city in the nation that can stage a festival of this magnitude without hosting a riot as well.

Tourists who were beginning to think of New Orleans as a place to avoid at Carnival believed it to be at its worst during this season. National publicity has demonstrated that New Orleanians are at their best during Carnival. Visitors bent on disorder are "discouraged" by local citizens.

After Bob Hope presented his Bacchus special to prime time millions, Mayor Moon Landrieu wrote Pip Brennan to say that New Orleans could neither buy nor pay for the positive image gained by the city on national television. Coming a month after the infamous Howard Johnson sniper tragedy, the show served to heal the black eye created by some of the live television coverage of the incident.

It would be misleading to make it appear that launching the krewe was all peaches and cream, a snap. To so imply would be like the kindergartener looking at the classroom ceiling in the hope that his wet pants are only a bad dream—all the while feeling the reality of soggy discomfort.

Before touching briefly on the unusual obstacles faced by Bacchus, it should be emphasized that members from all krewes were in support of the new idea. The Krewe of Rex, for example, whose captain thought well of the Bacchus plan, permitted Kern to store some of his materials in its dens so that the float builder might make room in one of his warehouses to begin work on Bacchus floats. Only a handful of powerful men from the inner circles of several old-line krewes were opposed.

When word circulated that a new krewe was being organized, there were rumblings about the planned format. But so many false starts had been made by well-intentioned people, Bacchus was not taken seriously. Fine.

To house its unusually large floats, Bacchus decided to build its own den. Some two months before Mardi Gras, 1969, a group of wives from the upper echelons of a major krewe, while visiting the office of the float designer and builder, stumbled upon the massive Bacchus floats under construction. "My Gawd, whose are these?"

The answer precipitated a meeting called, within days of the unscheduled preview, by members of the "inner circle" to discuss with members of Bacchus the horrid manner in which the new krewe was going to hurt Mardi Gras—how commercialism was going to get a toe-hold—a celebrity king from without the ranks and without community status was going to tear down proud traditions. Keeping the best bite for last, they pointed out that the celebrity king might foreshadow the accepted King of Carnival.

Coming from those few who believe their krewes are doing the "people" a favor by parading for their edification on the way to their grand balls, the exhortations glanced ineffectively off the armor of the determined Bacchus representatives who felt and still feel that the people are doing the krewes a favor by making their parades successful. Ever see a parade without spectators? Dull, dull, dull. Like running a feature film in an empty movie house.

Bacchus subsequently suffered a few cold shoulders—slights, if you will. When members were given the distinct impression the krewe would not be permitted to rent tractors and flambeaux lights from the usual source, leaders decided to purchase twenty tractors and construct their own rolling illumination, generators with four mercury lights at $1,000 each. Internal revenue considerations dictated that Blaine Kern purchase the tractors instead, but a point had been made ever so bluntly. Surely, the inner circle could take the budding krewe seriously now. For Kern, the tractor purchase turned into a successful satellite enterprise operating today as New Orleans Tractors, Inc.

One of the krewe's troubles was purely political. Dick Brennan recalls the parade permit episode vividly:

> Probably reflecting mounting pressure from aristocrats, the city was not overly anxious to grant a permit for the proposed parade. So zealous new krewe disciples buttonholed their respective councilmen unrelentingly prior to their consideration of the permit application.
>
> By virtue of his power base and social associations, one councilman was appraised as a probable negative vote; he was not contacted.
>
> When the measure was brought before the council, sure 'nuf, he objected. Seeing everyone else in favor, he appealed for a delay in the vote. "Could the police handle a Sunday night parade?" When assured that it could, he said he would vote for passage only after he had been given personal confirmation by the police chief himself. Another stall for time. His confidence that the item

> would be postponed until the next meeting melted like cold whipped cream on hot Irish coffee when Marshall Pearce escorted into the Council Chamber the police chief who had been waiting outside. Vote: 7-0. In the absence of Mayor Victor Schiro, Councilman Moon Landrieu signed the council action into law on the following morning. There would be a Bacchus parade.

Other obstacles were simply social. For years, a traditional pausing point for toasting of dignitaries by royalty of Canal-bound parades has been in front of a well-known Canal Street club. But during the first four years of Bacchus, members and guests were indelibly conspicuous by their total absence from reviewing stands; the club's lights were dark in apparent dissent. Only when Bob Hope came as Bacchus V did the famous club's stands fill up. Lights blazed like a hundred miniature suns.

Bacchus was accepted!

"Omnia mutantur, nos et mutamus in illis. All things change, and we change with them."—Matthias Borbonus. Amen!

Born the son of Zeus and Semeles, Bacchus was still an infant when his mother was killed by lightning. Zeus saved the child from the flames and enclosed him in his own thigh until he reached maturity. Thus it was said that Bacchus was twice born.

Thanks to co-captains Pip and Dick Brennan, the eleven other visionaries, and over 250 charter members, the god of wine was being resurrected, if not born a second time.

Bacchanals.

CHAPTER TWO

Danny "Bacchus" Kaye

A Reign of Unbounded Love and Laughter

In the pre-Bacchus era, Carnival kings were invariably local citizens, of Gentile persuasion, who perched on their parade thrones as courtiers tossed "throws" to the crowds.

Bacchus I lived in Beverly Hills, California, followed the Jewish faith, and personally tossed bushels of beads and doubloons to outstretched hands.

No stereotyped king, this Bacchus.

Danny Kaye, clearly elated at being selected to reign as the first Bacchus, came into town proclaiming that there be "unbounded love and laughter."

Kaye, ambassador-at-large for the United Nations Children's Fund, immediately established his intense interest in the little ones. As if to cover his tracks with the adult krewe members, he emphasized, "There are no adults. Adults make the best children." He would soon see how right he was.

Until the Sixties, Kaye had felt so strongly about his public image as related to his UNICEF work, he had consistently refused to play Las Vegas despite record offers from the desert resort. Yet here he was in New Orleans, at no charge. Only his travel expenses (as would be the policy for all Bacchus kings) would be reimbursed.

"Regardless of a person's age, he still retains some of the childhood traits for enjoying fun," Kaye proclaimed. He received no argument from the highly exuberant committee members meeting him at the airport. Asked if he wanted anything to drink, the comedian quickly quipped, "No, I wouldn't; let the District Attorney start his drilling."

Jacob and Clara Nemerovsky's son, reportedly withdrawn offstage, clearly considered himself onstage as his parade got underway.

Mirth-loving Bacchus led his floats through the streets and toasted from a goblet which replaced the usual king's sceptre. Garnished with grapes and pink trappings, his royal throne revolved on a pedestal.

PAGEANT OF
KREWE OF
BACCHUS
The Best Things in Life
1969
MARDI GRAS

Danny Kaye, Bacchus I, hams it up.

BACCHUS

The tailor's son looked heavier than most had expected. No calorie problem. Krewe bookkeeper Aurelia Frentz remembers that the thin, cold-natured king was visibly distressed at spending a couple of hours on a float during the penetrating February night. He was almost adamant about being provided with an electric blanket, Blaine Kern recalls. "With no receptacle to accommodate a blanket, I told him the old story about the electric car's advantages but extensions were not long enough. He didn't think it was funny at all." A compromise was reached as Bacchus I was sealed into a thick suit of thermal underwear to brave the cutting humid air.

Snags were few. Krewe members' fears that the larger-than-usual animated floats would encounter difficulty rounding the corner at Royal and Orleans never materialized. Officials of St. Louis Cathedral graciously permitted temporary removal of its historic hitching posts, thereby allowing Bacchus floats to roll upon the "banquettes." Rolling hydraulic jacks were fabricated for use in the event trouble developed, but fortunately were never needed.

An interview with the first king.

Concern that Kaye would be a dull prima donna king proved groundless. Alfred Bester has said, "No one in the history of entertainment has achieved Danny's casual control of audience." It was a power in awesome evidence on Sunday, February 16, 1969. The city of New Orleans was his theater, his audience in firm grasp.

Following the king's float, two Bacchanalian clown heads adorned the title float of the parade themed "The Best Things in Life." Two girls energetically stomped grapes in a vat on the third float, entitled simply "Wine." Huge champagne bottles bedecked the scene. Float No. 4, "Women," sported a boudoir with an alluring bathing beauty and other pretties surrounded by perfume, roses, and powder puffs. A white haired maestro conducted a symphony of colors on Float No. 5, "Music." Trumpets, harps, and piano keyboards were featured.

On the sixth float, the New Orleans Saints and the Buccaneers were given tribute on a float titled "Sports." In the float that followed, "Travel," a suitcase-carrying tourist grinned amidst a setting of travel folders while a globe advertised widespread destinations.

The eighth float, "Knowledge," featured books, diplomas, and other paraphernalia signifying lore and learning. "Health" was the theme of the ninth float, which showed a flexing muscleman displaying his power to a beach beauty. Among a conglomeration of artists, brushes, frames, and paintings, came Float No. 10, titled "Art."

One of the best things in life, especially in New Orleans, is "Food," depicted in Float No. 11 by chefs ministering to large hams, a turkey stuffed for the oven, the head of a steer, fruits, and vegetables. "Religion" was the theme of the next float garnished with the accouterments of worship—huge skulls, Christians and crosses, Buddhas, Krishnas, the Star of David, stone tablets, scrolls and totem poles.

On the thirteenth float, "Hunting" was represented by a jungle safari scene with lions and leopards. A young couple embracing on a swing as Cupid swirled overhead was featured on Float No. 14. Pink clouds, valentines, and sweetheart inscriptions were among the trappings of "Romance."

Co-captain "Pip" Brennan dressed up for the occasion.

Co-captain Dick Brennan dons Bacchus outfit.

A bevy of beautiful ladies receive a toast.

A toast to several hundred thousand Bacchanals.

"Patriotism" came as the last float, complete with Uncle Sam, the Statue of Liberty, and the Stars and Stripes, as well as a cannon, flares, rockets, firecrackers, and pinwheel.

Bacchus had promised bigger, better, more animated floats. And Bacchus had delivered. Or at least, the *Times-Picayune* of the following morning thought it had:

> In a Carnival season filled with maiden voyages for parades, Bacchus made the biggest splash of all Sunday night.
>
> The brash newcomer had promised the biggest floats ever—bigger than Rex—and some exciting ideas in animation.
>
> Bacchus didn't exaggerate. The floats were outstanding.
>
> And the crowds, which turned out at six deep along the entire parade route despite temperatures in the mid-40s and brisk winds, seemed to agree that Bacchus had lived up to his promise.
>
> "I hear this parade is supposed to be something special" was a regular comment from seasoned Carnival veterans as they waited to give Bacchus his chance. And invariably as the floats went by, the "show me" veterans agreed with one man who said, "This is really good and it's different."
>
> In fact, in many sections the crowd was so interested in watching the huge, animated floats and admiring the costumes that the traditional scramble for beads and doubloons was considerably subdued.
>
> And with the average of 20 maskers tossing throws from a float, there was plenty to scramble for.
>
> In fulfilling its promise to create a new and better Carnival parade, Bacchus also broke tradition by having Kaye, a non-resident of New Orleans, as its king.
>
> Kaye took the precedent one step further by throwing beads to the crowds himself.
>
> That just isn't done, but the crowd loved it.
>
> The next move is yours, Rex.

Some 1600 merrymakers had a ball at the rendezvous afterwards. Ralph Flanagan's Band played. Krewe members played. Their guests—not to be relegated to the traditional "call out" section or less—played.

Like Hans Christian Andersen's children, Danny Kaye's grown up little ones played.

The Age of Bacchus had begun.

Royalty.

CHAPTER THREE

Raymond "Bacchus" Burr

Guilty on All Counts

Actor Raymond Burr, a big man in many ways, was crowned Bacchus II. A charitable person, he contributes selflessly to his two primary causes célèbre: 1. Fund-raising efforts for and morale boosting of paraplegics. (His confinement to "Ironsides' " wheelchair has given him a sensitive affinity for the severely handicapped whom he spends countless hours visiting in hospitals around the country.) 2. Support of justice, law and order—an interest inspired by two successful television series, "Perry Mason" and "Ironsides."

Also mammoth in physical dimension, the jovial, piercing-blue-eyed Canadian—what, a foreign king?—was a hulk of a man at the time, tipping Toledo at over 300 pounds.

"Convincing Burr to serve as Bacchus was probably easier than any other king," Dick Brennan recalls. "I had met him on the way to pre-revolution Cuba in the 1950s, and grew to know him better with each of his numerous trips to his favorite city—New Orleans. He loves our city and particularly its jazz. When he's in town, we always hit the spots like the Paddock Lounge and Famous Door. Anyway, he had become a fast friend of the family, and all it took was one call from Ella (Brennan)."

After a brief explanation of the Bacchus concept, Burr replied, "You want me, you got me."

Big Daddy Ray was quite popular on television at the time of his elevation to godhood, and the reverence exhibited by well-wishers reflected a wide recognition factor, as they say in political opinion polls.

While Danny thrilled the 1969 crowd with the nimble dance, poignant pantomime, and mad mimicry that are his trademarks, Burr could hardly captivate the crowd with a courtroom scene. And so he relied on the basic attribute of his Greek namesake—a dynamic, engaging, forceful personality.

BACCHUS

Every reign brings its share of humorous incidents, and Burr's was typical. While the celebrity was changing into his royal robes before the parade and at the Rivergate rendezvous that followed, a dapper chap in tails chatted with the king and attended to his every need. Sir Gallant turned out to be an imposter. While krewe members were under the impression that the man was Burr's friend, the king in turn believed him to be a member of the krewe assigned to assist him.

"Remember When" was the theme of the second annual Bacchus parade. Nineteen floats, presenting scenes ranging from Lucky Lindy's flight to the Roaring Twenties and the Great Depression, snaked through the ocean of onlookers who flooded sidewalks, curbs, ladders, and porches and perched in windows and trees.

From Washington via St. Charles to Canal, to Elks Place, down Rampart to Orleans, then onto Royal and back on Canal to the blast at Rivergate . . . the parade inched along. Hundreds of thousands of parade watchers served as Ironsides' judge and jury. The verdict: guilty!—of bringing joy, laughter and exhilaration to Carnival and status to the growing new krewe.

Coming after several days and nights of parties honoring the god-to-be, a two- to three-hour Bacchus parade can be taxing on the system unless the king paces himself. Burr gave so much to his role and to his constituents that he appeared near exhaustion when his float reached its terminus.

Floatbuilder Kern relates this anecdote: "When it came time to defloat in Rivergate, Bacchus II looked around perplexedly for the ladder. Finding it was easy; negotiating the undersized contraption was another matter. Like a newborn chick who doesn't quite know how to escape his sticky shell, he hesitated at the head of the tiny rungs that would support his solid frame to the floor below. Finally he spotted me in the sea of faces and motioned for assistance." Blaine placed his hands under his majesty's arms and prayed for supernatural strength. Kern's prayers went unanswered as Burr missed the last two rungs and came thundering like Father Zeus onto his benefactor—pounding him to his knees in the perilous process.

The star of "Godzilla, King of the Monsters" had almost relegated Blaine to one of his television series wheelchairs. Henceforth it was decreed, not by a proclamation from Mount Olympus but by a resolution from the board of directors, that a forklift would be purchased to use in evacuating rollicking royalty from the floats. And Blaine would long ponder the wisdom of the TV producer who had named the rotund actor's series "Ironsides."

Continually toasting his worshipers, a towering figure of Bacchus stood on the King's float while a Dixieland band played jazz favorites at the front.

Two Bacchanalian clowns grinned at each other from each end of the theme float, "Remember When." Beneath a revolving crown, a light-flashing marquee announced the scenario to follow.

The third float, "School Days," portrayed the old school marm rolling her eyes and turning her head from side to side as she taught reading, writing, and arithmetic.

"Our First Childhood Sweetheart" followed on float four with two lovers

Hey, it fits!

A crown of grapes.

Title float—"Remember When."

riding high above the crowd on a bicycle built for two. Spinning madly while Cupid shot his arrows of love at everyone was a large Catherine wheel of hearts.

The fifth float remembered "The First Cars." One was driven by two old-fashioned motorists in goggles and dusters.

Perry and Byrd explored the poles on Float No. 6. Frozen wastes of the Arctic were sculptured in brilliant turquoise aquamarine. Royal blue added color to the white float. Admiral Byrd planted the United States flag at the pole.

Float No. 7 portrayed "The Good Ole Summertime" with a large sun smiling and blinking as rays turned about its head. Wheels turned and smoke puffed as New Orleans' favorite train, Smoky Mary, chugged along.

A giant minister performed nuptial rites on the next float entitled "On Our Wedding Day." A huge silver and white wedding cake topped by a bride and groom turned slowly.

"The Daring Hero, Lucky Lindy" followed on Float No. 9. The year was 1927 and Charles Lindbergh headed east toward Europe and fame with his *Spirit of St. Louis*.

Featuring a large, animated ringmaster in top hat, float ten presented an imposing life-size elephant peering down at the crowd. Theme: "When the Circus Comes to Town."

"Armistice Day" was featured on Float No. 11. With helmet cocked to the

Rivergate rendezvous.

crowd, a smiling doughboy rolled his eyes as two cannons belched flames and smoke into the February air.

Float No. 12 was named "The Fantastic Roaring 20s." A typical "guys and dolls" gangster grimaced as he held his hands high at gunpoint.

The next float portrayed the great Depression. "Bank Closed," "WPA," and "CCC" signs abounded as the monster, "Poverty," lunged out at the crowd.

On the fourteenth float, the principal was Charlie Chaplin in "Hollywood and the Silver Screen." Charlie rolled his eyes, twitched his mustache and turned his head from side to side.

In "An Old-Fashioned Christmas" on Float No. 15, Santa rode his reindeer-drawn sleigh high above the crowd while snowflakes floated among blue and white clouds.

"The Golden Age of Sports," on Float No. 16, had the "Bambino," Babe Ruth, typifying the legends of his era in sports. Swinging his bat and moving his head from side to side, the "Yankee slugger" was backdropped by stadium-filled stands.

Float No. 17, "The Swing Years," had a monstrous jukebox flashing spectacular colors while a zootsuiter of that period gyrated wildly to the jukebox's music.

With Raymond Burr as Bacchus II, it was only natural that "The World of Television" be given its deserved place of prominence in recent history. A large television screen blinked off and on while various products were sold by a pair of large hands emanating from the evil eye.

Float No. 19 recalled "The Flower Children." A bare-chested hippie decorated with colorful beads extended his hand to the crowd while his "chick" sat amid a garden of flowers.

"Man's Conquest of Space" was depicted on the final float. An astronaut standing on the edge of a lunar crater brought the history lesson to a close.

At the dinner dance that followed, Bacchus II continued his celebration in the best of bacchanal tradition as Bob Crosby's "Bob Cats" entertained. Burr and his blue eyes captivated completely the distaff revelers.

Members left Rivergate that night knowing that the huge success of Bacchus I had not been a fluke. Bacchus was a winner again. Next year? Who could imagine?

CHAPTER FOUR

Jim "Bacchus" Nabors

Shazam!!

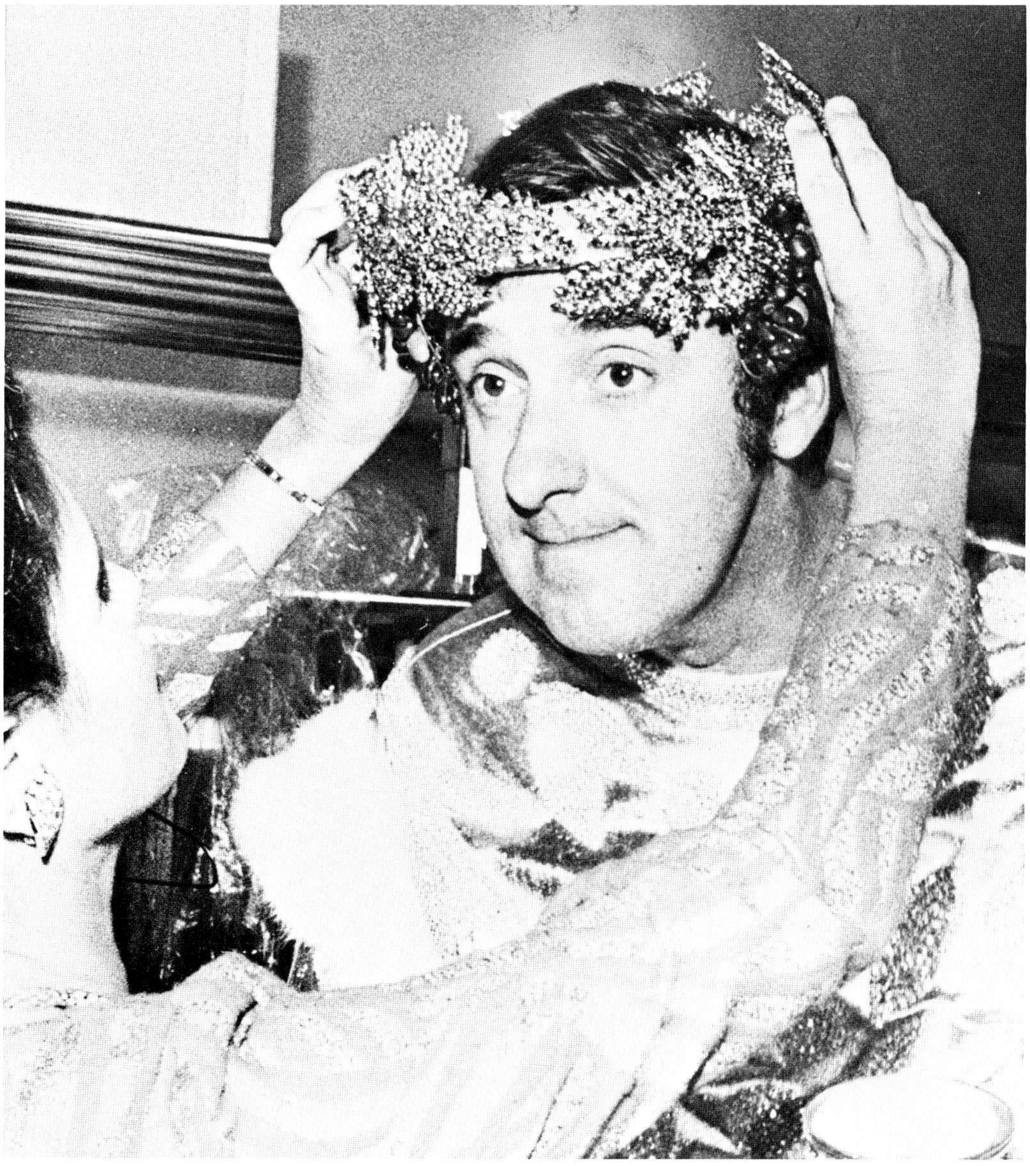

From court jester to crown sovereign.

BACCHUS

The krewe's determination to make the man, woman, and child on the street feel more a part of Carnival was accentuated with the selection of Jim Nabors as 1971 king. Other kings might relate as well with the crowds, but it would be hard to exceed the fervor with which revelers welcomed TV's most famous Marine, Gomer Pyle.

"I like you cuz you're common, everyday folks like me," was what the multitude of wellwishers seemed to be saying to the comedian–singer, who can be convincingly sophisticated when he drops his Alabama twang. The tumultuous roar of "Hey Gomer" widened the king's smile, already stretching from ear to ear. The Sylacauga, Alabama native responded to the cheers with teeth resembling the ivory of a baby grand.

Pip Brennan says Bacchus added a fine citizen to New Orleans in the person of Jim Nabors. "Every chance he gets, anytime he's in the vicinity, Jim makes a point of making it to New Orleans to partake of her uniqueness. He's one of our city's best salesmen."

For a while, it looked like an exorcist might have to be sought to purge the 1971 parade of its problems. As the king's float reached Gallier Hall, a fire erupted thereon. Luckily, a police unit near the float brought it quickly under control and extinguished it without any damage of consequence. Forty-mile-per-hour winds forced the krewe to trim the parade route, because the gigantic floats and riders might be endangered in the gale. A blaze on Bourbon Street and the resulting fire-fighting equipment blocked a segment of the originally planned parade route on Royal Street. Added to these near-demonic happenings was the injury of a person run over by a float at N. Peters and Gravier as the parade was disbanding.

But just as television's Gomer surmounted every obstacle imposed upon him by Sergeant Carter, so too did god Bacchus III ignore the problems around him. It was obvious that he was having one helluva good time aboard the lead float, covered with glittering gold canopies. The Pyle smile grew wider with each passing block.

The traditional harlequin beamed a broad smile toward a field of scrolls and rising theater curtains on the second float, while a marquee flashed the parade theme, "Bacchus Salutes Mardi Gras." Uninformed late-comers to the parade must have thought Carnival spirits had finally done them in when they saw a convincing portrayal of "Rex, King of Carnival" on the third float. "I thought it was Sunday but it must be Tuesday," a wino from Camp Street could be imagined muttering to himself.

On Float No. 4, Bacchus paid tribute to the Krewe of Comus, the oldest of all Carnival clubs.

Mecca came next with an animated genie rising from a magic lamp while colorful mosques portrayed the beauty of the exotic city.

Float No. 6 presented Hermes, winged messenger of the gods. He sped through the heavens with his chariot traversing a vast field of planets, moons, and comets.

An Indian princess sitting among flowers, vines, and trees was the setting for Chief Choctaw on the seventh float.

Proteus, who has the power to appear as anything he dang well chooses, was aboard Float No. 8 as a giant silver sprite rising from ocean depths.

Atlas was on Float No. 9 as a gigantic statue supporting the world on its shoulders.

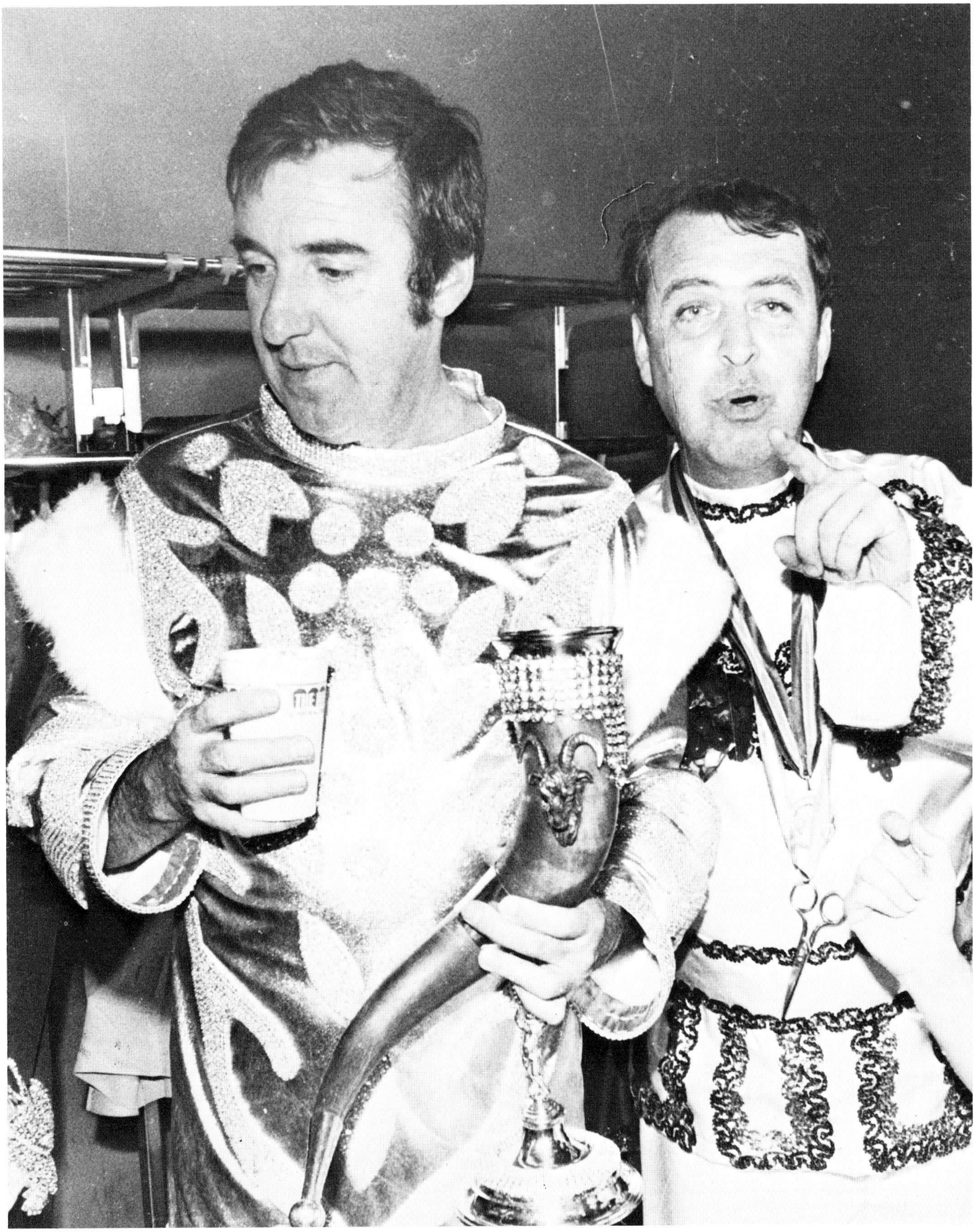

Suiting up–Jim Nabors and Larry Youngblood, charter member and costume designer.

Okeanos.

Charter member-chariot rider, Pete Moss.

Throw me something, mister.

Neighborly Nabors grins obligingly, flanked by the junior Owen Brennans (far left and second from right), and the Blaine Kerns (far right and second from left).

King Sargon's palace, replete with hanging gardens, was colorfully depicted on Float 10, while the large jester symbolizing the Knights of Babylon displayed the high spirits of the vivacious krewe.

Momus, God of Ridicule, came next, sitting atop billowing clouds on Float No. 11. A backdrop of "heroic" Roman architecture arched skyward as Momus repeated his "Dum Vivimus, Vivimus! While We Live, Let Us Live!"

Human skulls hanging from trees were part of the jungle scene wherein the soul Krewe of Zulu cavorted in the African jungles of Float No. 12.

Paying tribute to the Krewe of Venus, graceful swans attended a statue of Venus de Milo, Goddess of Love, on Float No. 13.

On Float No. 14, the Egyptian God of Wisdom and Magic, Thoth, stood with arms crossed before his temple. A pharoah worshipped at the altar.

On Float No. 15, Endymion, Greek God of Youth, was represented by a large figure in enchanting woodlands, as a crescent moon beamed contentedly upon the scene.

BACCHUS

The heroic son of Jupiter, Hercules, engaged in his work as many-headed Hydra rose from the center of the scene on Float No. 16.

Looking down from Olympus, on the seventeenth float was Zeus, father of Bacchus and chairman of the board of Olympian gods. Lightning, released by his mighty power, streaked across the skies.

Float No. 18 paid tribute to Pandora as an opened box revealed the various problems haunting mankind.

The God of Streams and Rivers, Okeanos, rode the waves on a chariot drawn by a fish-tailed horse. A menacing octopus complemented a colorful coral reef scene.

At the rendezvous that followed the parade, Count Basie thrilled music lovers while Nabors entertained the crowd, visited tables, autographed programs. He seemed deeply moved by the honor of serving as Bacchus. "I really don't know how to act like a king," he said. "In all the high school shows I was ever in, I was never so much as a prince. . . . Someone asked me last night what I was going to think about while perched up on top of that float. I thought for a while and then answered her by saying, that I will just be thinking how lucky I am to be up here. You know, it's a shame you can't in some way bottle this spirit and use it later when ever you want."

On the night preceding the parade, Nabors sang "Dixie" from his Bourbon Street balcony to a crowd gathered below. This part of Dixie would long remember his participation in the Carnival of Carnivals.

"I used to come to New Orleans with about two bucks in my pocket," he said. "But I had never seen Mardi Gras before, and now I can say that one word describes it—fantastic!" Ditto for Jim's visit.

He would return to ride with his successors.

BACCHUS IN COLOR

Bob Hope, Bacchus the Great.

Jim Nabors, Bacchus III, salutes Mardi Gras.

Bacchus IV has crown fitting.

Danny Kaye, Bacchus I.

Pegasus.

Momus.

Monsters in review.

Atlas.

Bacchus III theme float.

Bacchusaurus.

Theme float.

High Noon.

Cleopatra.

Walt Disney.

Gone with the Wind.

Planet of the Apes.

True Grit.

Goldfinger.

CHAPTER FIVE

Phil "Bacchus" Harris

That's What I Like About the South

Epitome of the royal stance.

In 1973, Bacchus V (Bob Hope) would refer to Bacchus IV (Phil Harris) as having "the wettest reign." Bacchus Hope would also label Phil Harris the only king who floated off his float. Jovial Phil left nothing to the unrestrained New Orleans imagination, particularly his facile dominance of Queen Alcohol. "This guy taught Dean Martin what little he knows about drinking," an observing Bacchus member offered.

Two kingships previous, Raymond Burr had neglected to pace himself and suffered 'smashing' consequences. Phil refused to likewise pace himself, but it didn't show. "Perhaps his unpaced pace is his usual pace," the Bacchant proposed. His performance brought to mind one of Jack Benny's famous jokes: When someone at the dinner table referred to Phil Harris, Benny pleaded, "Please! Not while we're eating."

"Book of Horrors" doubloon.

With the elevation of Harris to king, traditionalists who had thought ill of the out-of-town kings must have felt appeased. Finally, they thought, the krewe had seen the light in selecting a New Orleanian. Wrong! Harris only acts like a native. He was born in 1906 in Linton, Indiana, but grew up in Nashville, Tennessee. Only in the course of falling in love with the Crescent City did he adopt the lady as his hometown.

The bandleader–sidekick who performed for over a decade on the Jack Benny Show confides he would like to live in New Orleans but worries that he wouldn't be loved as much if he became a resident. "I couldn't take that," he desponds.

When Al Hirt performs in New York, Washington, Chicago or on the West Coast, people idolize him, Harris explains. At his club on Bourbon Street, however, he's just ole Al to local folks. He's not the proverbial out-of-town expert.

A frequent television variety show guest, the easy-going comedian does have a direct blood tie with New Orleans. His daughter is married to Doug Regan, Bacchus charter member and one of the conceivers of the krewe concept.

Ruled by a star of "The High and the Mighty," the Bacchus IV dynasty could have with all logic been pegged the same—Harris was "high" and his reception was "mighty" close to being unbelievable. Indulging himself during every minute of the annual celebration, Bacchus IV swayed not once—at least not noticeably. He simply planted both feet on the floor of the float and, like an old lady standing in a rolling, rocking St. Charles streetcar, absorbed all of the action in the knees.

Capturing elicitly the color of the evening, the *States-Item* of the following morning put it thusly:

> Bacchus, the god of wine and merriment, thundered into the French Quarter late last night, and trundled out of the record crowds there well after midnight.
>
> Maskers on the mammoth, kinetic, electric floats people have come to associate with Bacchus, shoveled seeming tons of doubloons, beads and giddiness to the throngs. [T]his year, the floats depicted . . . monsters.
>
> The parade itself began with the usual pomp and libation as entertainer Phil Harris, known for the night as Bacchus IV, toasted and sang his way down St. Charles, through the Quarter and into the Rivergate convention center.
>
> The parade began with a bevy of gorillas, one of them King Kong, carrying the traditional woman in his paws, and the animation would have done a Disney proud.

PHIL "BACCHUS" HARRIS

The between float spaces were generously interspersed with delights . . . boisterous bands . . . people wearing papier-mâché crazyheads . . . huge brewery horses . . . people on standard horseback . . . rag-tag devil-may-care flambeaux toters.

The parade over, the Quarter remained blanketed with humanity, and with the smell of sweet "pop" wine on its glass-strewn streets.

And New Orleans went to bed wondering what was going to happen at this rate, come Mardi Gras.

After the King's float, floats No. 2 and 3 together read, "Bacchus Presents—Bacchus' Book of Horrors." The presentation on the remaining floats was as follows:

No. 4, King Kong; No. 5, The Mummy; No. 6, The Werewolf; No. 7, Cyclops; No. 8, Witches and Goblins; No. 9, The Hunchback of Notre Dame; No. 10, Space Monster.

Jazzing it up with Lou Sano.

Floats previewed at open house.

Giving "Book of Horrors" theme a hand.

From the Bacchus "Book of Horrors."

No. 11, Dracula; No. 12; Creature from the Black Lagoon; No. 13, Dr. Jekyll and Mr. Hyde; No. 14, Fu Manchu, No. 15, Abominable Snowman; No. 16, The Devil; No. 17, Jack the Ripper; No. 18, Godzilla; No. 19, Phantom of the Opera; and Float No. 20, Frankenstein, of course.

At the dinner dance afterward, Harry James provided his hallmark sounds to the electrifying melee which has come to be known as the Bacchus Rendezvous. King Harris continued to entertain.

Did Phil Harris truly enjoy himself, or was he acting to please the crowd? His return to New Orleans to participate in the reigns of Bacchus V and VI should be sufficient answer.

Like Miss America, a Bacchus king traditionally carries the title until his successor ascends his throne the following year. Come next February, Harris would pester Bob Hope unrelentingly during the days preceding the parade. Only with the crowning of good King Bob would "the wettest reign" come to an official end.

A pinch of "Stardust" from Harry James.

Smile, Alice, you're standing next to a god.

Bob Hope.

CHAPTER SIX

Bob "Bacchus" Hope

Thanks for the Memories

For many kings, history carved out a niche of some import. Then, only once in a long while would a king surface with such impact that his title proclaimed his greatness—Alexander the Great of Macedonia, Peter the Great of Russia, Charlemagne ("Charles the Great") of the Holy Roman Empire, etc.

Few will dispute that Kings Danny Kaye, Raymond Burr, Jim Nabors, and Phil Harris reigned with distinction in the young realm of Bacchus. However, even the five preceding monarchs would surely agree that it was Bacchus V who should be designated "Bacchus the Great."

More than once, Bob Hope had been invited to be god Bacchus, but because dates conflicted with his Desert Golf Classic, the krewe's impossible dream had not materialized. On one occasion, the giant of giants in the entertainment world had replied that, although he could not accept, he was scheduled to be flying over New Orleans on Bacchus Sunday and would wave. Funny, but of little consolation.

Dreaming you're in the arms of your lover can be stimulating, but waking up to find you're actually entwined . . . well! The Krewe of Bacchus learned, almost unbelievably, in the fall of 1972 that Bob Hope would indeed serve as Bacchus V. It was no longer a dream. The then 70-year-old author of "Have Tux, Will Travel" was ready to travel to an experience he would forever remember.

A series of letters followed, which are printed below. Of interest is the penciled notation on the letter of January 10, 1973—"20 rooms." On January 25 the notation reads "45 rooms instead of twenty"—the king's entourage is growing.

The one and only . . . Bob Hope.

November 11, 1972

Mr. Owen E. Brennan, Jr. and
Mr. Richard Brennan
417 Royal Street
New Orleans, Louisiana 70130

Dear Brennans:

I also am looking forward to being King Bacchus this coming March.

I'm also trying to arrange for a TV commitment, so we can get us some national exposure.

My measurements are 42-36-36. Sounds a little like Raquel, but it's true. I'll have Bill Faith send you profile pictures.

I think it might be fun if you would fly out here with the films, and show Dolores and me what really goes on down there. Maybe we're too old for this type of work.

I'll be in touch.

Regards,

/S/

BOB

BH;ik

November 30, 1972

Owen E. Brennan, Jr.
417 Royal Street
New Orleans, Louisiana 70130

Dear Owen:

Glad you received the measurements. Don't believe them — they may change any minute.

I think it would be a good idea if you would come out some time in January because I'm really chilled as far as my schedule is concerned before that. But I would like you to come out with the films so that Dolores could see them and we could discuss the show.

I know you're going to be very happy to hear that the films that we take down there of the Mardi Gras will be on my show on March 7th for Ford. So we'll get a lot of exposure and we're going to have to work out a practical schedule so we can film everything before that time.

I'll be in touch with you. Good to hear from you.

Regards,

/S/

BOB

BH;mh

10346 Moorpark St.
North Hollywood
California 91602

January 10, 1973

Mr. Owen Brennan, Jr.
c/o Brennan's
417 Royal Street
New Orleans, Louisiana 70130

Dear Owen:

As a follow up to our telephone conversation the other day regarding Bob Hope, as I mentioned, Bob has agreed to be King Bacchus V and, with the understanding that the parade is on March 4th, we are making arrangements to tape or film his television show in New Orleans on March 1, 2 and 3. We will undoubtedly utilize a number of the personalities who will be in New Orleans during that period for the program.

Would it be possible for you to advise whether Bob will be needed for any affairs other than the parade itself? In other words, if he must attend some functions prior to the fourth, we will have to try and work our television schedule around them.

Bob still thinks it might be a good idea if he could see the film so that he will have a general idea of what takes place during this period. Is it possible to send the film without your having to make the trip along with it?

Also, as I mentioned in passing, when Bob tapes his television shows there is a substantial crew, between the production end and the technicians. Will we have a problem getting accommodations for up to twenty people at that time?

Please let me hear from you.

Very truly yours,

/S/

John F. Dugan

20 rooms

Mr. Owen Brennan, Jr.
Brennan's
417 Royal Street
New Orleans, Louisiana 70130

Dear Owen:

Attached hereto is a costume sheet with all of Bob Hope's measurements.

We are still working on a location to do the Television Show. As soon as it is set up, I will advise.

Also, there is no determination as yet about showing him the film. I will be in touch with you about this.

All good wishes,

/S/

John F. Dugan

January 25, 1973

45 rooms instead of twenty

Wait 'till Bing sees this.

If the reign of Phil Harris was the wettest, Hope's rule was destined to be the funniest. From prompt arrival to late departure, the comedian lived up to and exceeded expectations.

It was fitting that an arrival party for the king and his friends be thrown at Adelaide Brennan's home, where six years previous thirteen young men had met to nudge a dream to reality. Phil Harris was present at the affair and he and Bob Hope tangled for over an hour of wisecracks. The two long-time friends dug deep into their bag of one-liners, some from as far back as the 1930s. Reminded of the fact that he was king until the actual crowning of his successor, Phil croaked, "You mean I'm still god?"

Bob entertained the assembly with many of the great lines which had

Being king is great, but do I have to have a jester?

nurtured the Hope legend. "I went out to my old grammar school yesterday," he reminisced. "There was the same old desk, the same old inkwell, the same old shaving kit." Wife Dolores was enticed to sing a number or two but preferred to stay in the comfortable background, obviously taken in by the whole affair but content in the shadow of the monument. "Of course, Dolores is much too good for me. She was raised on the right side of the tracks. We Hopes were raised under the tracks."

Actually Leslie Townes Hope was born in Eltham, Kent, England in 1903, arrived at Ellis Island in 1908, and was reared in Cleveland. By his teens, he had teamed up with a friend to form a smalltime act around Cleveland known as "Songs, Patter, Eccentric Dancing." A half century later he would be king of comedians, prince to American servicemen, and god of Bacchus.

As the parade hour approached, krewe members tensed. Word buzzed around that Bob was not to be found. Out for an afternoon of golf with Dick Brennan at the New Orleans Country Club, the cool, calm, hooked duffer was trying to complete 18 holes when his driver reminded him of the late hour. A mad ride in a limousine borrowed from the Fontainebleau Motor Hotel delivered the great profile to Rivergate with barely enough time to suit up.

With this, the funniest Bacchus, even some of the serious events turned out to be hilarious. A case in point: well into the parade route, champagne agitated a slight kidney ailment, producing severe discomfort for the king and a need to locate a bathroom. When Hope advised Blaine Kern of the impending emergency, the float builder broke into a cold sweat. Stunned by the prospect of stopping a 23-float parade, marching bands, and motor escorts, Blaine stalled for time. A few minutes later, Hope matter-of-factly asked Blaine if it was permissible for a king to wet his royal robes, his throne, and float. Blaine knew a precedent was about to be set.

Word was passed down the line that the parade would be halted momentarily. In front of the Hotel Orleans on Canal St., the king's float stopped. A three-wheeler motorcycle was parked alongside to help him step down. Kern, a wedge of policemen and two 300-pound tractor drivers surrounded the king and plowed through a yelling, grabbing, shoving crowd of worshipers. Through the lobby and into a waiting elevator, the king and his makeshift court swarmed like worker bees after their queen. When the elevator door closed, Blaine turned to see Bacchus V pinned against the back wall, hands above head, with no room to lower either. Doors opened and they raced down the hall to the bathroom.

Fait accompli, the expedition descended back to the lobby. Word had spread that Bob had entered the hotel to toast someone. Rumors, rumors, rumors. Outside, the estimated 2,000 pressing, pushing, pawing admirers stretched to touch their god, Bacchus. The wedge plowed ever so slowly through the near-riotous uproar until Bob made his way back to the three-wheeler and awkwardly up to the safety of the float. In so doing, his position revealed an opened rear zipper and the underlying thermal underwear. Believing this to be part of the comedian's act, the crowd roared. Turning to Blaine, a relieved Hope said, "I don't think it was worth it; I'm convinced it would have been better to wet my pants."

Adoration of Bacchus the Great.

Bob the Great performs.

With that pronouncement, the parade resumed its way among the largest, loudest, merriest multitude of people a Bacchus had ever witnessed. Close to a million, it was estimated.

Bob Hope thought he had seen it all—on his travels around the world, in his junkets to entertain troops in three wars, from the White House to the Kremlin, New York to London's Palladium. He even once traded ad-libs with the king of England—"The only time I ever had a king for a straight man." Tonight Bob was king, and his power rivaled the lightning bolts of Father Zeus. In dazed disbelief, the Grand Marshall of two Rose Bowl parades said, "I thought I had seen everything, but this is adoration."

New Orleans Mayor Moon Landrieu gives his view of the proceedings.

Mayor Landrieu observes as Washington Redskins quarterback Billy Kilmer offers Hope a spot on his "over the hill" team.

Wow! This coffee and chickory goes to your head!.

BACCHUS

As if to accentuate the fact that Bob Hope didn't need publicity, the Monday, March 5 *States-Item* devoted less than three inches of copy to the previous evening's Bacchus parade, and those twenty-three lines were sandwiched between Proteus and Thoth.

> Yesterday began with showers but the skies cleared by midmorning, providing perfect weather for six parades.
>
> The biggest was Bacchus, which rolled last night with Bob Hope as Bacchus V. The comedian led a 23-float parade with the theme of "Bacchus Goes to the Movies." Police said the turnout was the largest in the history of Bacchus.
>
> The floats displayed scenes from such films as "Gone With The Wind," "True Grit," "The African Queen," and "The Road to Morocco," which Hope made with Bing Crosby.
>
> Serenaded by a jazz band, Hope sat on his float beneath a large cluster of grapes surrounding Bacchus' motto, "In Vino Veritas."
>
> The god of wine's parade provided a tumultuous climax to a day of parades.

The African Queen.

The Road to Morocco.

BACCHUS

Bob and Jill St. John rehearse for national network special on Bacchus.

Bob's old road shows were no match for his road show to Rivergate, where he proceeded to entertain the troops at a dinner dance filled to capacity with 4,000 bubbling Bacchants. Harry James played again; Pat Barberot served as back-up band.

A plane was kept waiting at Moisant for an hour and a half after its planned departure so that Bob could be aboard for his return to California where he would edit the television special taped prior and during the parade and dance.

On March 7, 50 million television viewers would know of Bacchus, of Carnival, of Mardi Gras. They would have an opportunity to see New Orleans as a friendly, safe, festive city.

Almost a quarter of the nation's citizenry would judge for itself whether or not the recent Howard Johnson sniper incident was actually a reflection of a sick city, as has been portrayed by some electronic mediamen. Or was it instead an isolated tragedy—admittedly made no less tragic by its isolation—that could plague any city, anywhere, anytime. Fifty million people might ponder the thought of hosting a similar festival in their respective cities without major outbreaks of violence.

At that time, Bob Hope was Number One insofar as television ratings were concerned. On that March evening, his audience was focused on the Crescent City—and it was all to the credit of a five-year-old Carnival krewe.

In Vino Veritas! In wine there is truth!

CHAPTER SEVEN

Glen "Bacchus" Campbell

By The Time I Get To Rivergate . . .

February nights were never like this in Delight, Arkansas.

At ease before the spectacle.

GLEN "BACCHUS" CAMPBELL

Bacchus is dedicated to giving the people a larger role in Carnival, and Delight, Arkansas' favorite son, Glen Campbell, was pleased with his part. He related with his subjects on somewhat the same "He's one of us" plane as had been the case with Jim Nabors.

Immediately upon arrival, the Good-Time-Hour star made it clear as Ozark mountain dew that he was at the krewe's service. "You tell me what you want me to do; point me in that direction, and I'll do it."

Campbell knew he was in high cotton in the exclusive club of big names—Kaye, Burr, Nabors, Harris, Hope. He took his part so seriously, he personally had his costume tailored to conform with Bacchus specifications, but modified slightly to suit his personality.

Like a little boy at the gum-ball machine, Bacchus VI knew from the start that this was going to be fun. Perennial participants, Nabors and Harris, were back in town to pay homage to their colleague and their adopted city. Also basking in the wanton revelry were the Smothers Brothers, a pair Glen

That's my costume? You've got to be kidding!

had helped propel to stardom when he hosted their summer television series in 1968. Among the other celebrities present were Dorothy Lamour, Ed Nelson, Yogi Berra, Rusty Staub.

Glen, oftentimes a below par golfer, was set to birdie every hole from the parade launch on St. Charles to the nineteenth hole at a romping Rivergate.

Accompanied on his float by a jazz band, Glen sang his way through sixty-four blocks of humanity which had come to accept the fact that Bacchus was one hundred percent guaranteed quality . . . sure success . . . an evening to remember.

At a pause in the parade, the youngest Bacchus leaned over and said to Blaine Kern, "For the greater part of my 18 years on the farm, I spent my time following a plow and staring at a mule's behind. Just witness what looking at the boob tube has done . . . how many friends it has created for me."

Yogi Berra, Danny Abramowicz, and spouses.

"Bacchus Reads the Comics" doubloon.

The parade was a 22-float extravaganza. Theme: "Bacchus Reads the Comics." Following the title float was Campbell enthroned among golden drapes and canopies.

Float No. 3 was Dick Tracy in a police action scene, with fast moving squad cars, blazing guns, and handcuffs.

On the fourth float, Al Capp's Li'l Abner was in his overalls being ministered to by a decolletéd Daisy Mae.

Following came the striking figure of Prince Valiant in armor, indulging in a toast at the king's pavillion.

On Float No. 7, Dennis the Menace dreamed up more mischief as Margaret spun on a pink flower.

Casper the Friendly Ghost, on Float No. 8, was comfortable in a cemetery scene.

On Float No. 9, Robin waited in readiness as Batman-in-leotards prepared for another adventure.

On the next float, Blondie and Dagwood were shown alongside their white frame house.

Float No. 11, Superman, the flying crime fighter, waited beside a telephone booth. Skyscrapers towered around him.

Observing a space ship that had landed near a rocket observation tower, Buck Rogers stood with raised gun on the next float.

Dressed in a flower-sprinkled miniskirt and brief top, Queen Kong applied makeup to interest her suitor on Float No. 13.

Wolfing a can of spinach to regain his strength on the fourteenth float was Popeye, the sailor man.

Mickey Mouse, along with Goofy, Pluto, and Donald Duck, bantered and bickered on the next float.

On Float No. 16, Bugs Bunny was trying to eat Elmer Fudd's tasty carrots. Meanwhile, Elmer searched about for the thief.

On the seventeenth float, half-dressed Beetle Bailey received a boot in the derriere from a superior officer.

As Mark Trail surveyed a clean environment, a sign reading "Give a Hoot, Don't Pollute" editorialized on Float No. 18.

Holding an ice cream cone for the missus as he paused in bewilderment outside Ye Old Pub was Andy Capp, on Float No. 19.

Float 20 hosted the Katzenjammer Kids playing in an area of trees and rocks. Two boldly colored parrots perched on a swing.

Standing before a temple with a Buddha statue at the entrance was Terry of Terry and the Pirates on Float 21.

The final float was King Kong. The gargantuan figure of the beast stood before chains and shackles, roaring defiance.

If the cooperative Bacchus VI extended himself to dole out entertainment and doubloons during the parade, he performed even better at the rendezvous. Acting as though he owed something to krewe members and guests for inviting him, the blue-eyed, four-time Emmy Award winner sang, cavorted, hopped from table to table signing autographs, kissing the ladies and shaking hands with their men. Duke Ellington, in one of his last major appearances, played with passion.

A Bacchus ball is a suave affair. Although it is wide open in participation compared to the traditional Carnival krewe ball, the elegant dresses, scintillating coiffures, all manner of formal men's wear, a big name band, lavish decorations, all add up to what Blaine Kern believes to be "the finest, most elaborate party thrown annually in the whole of these United States. I have attended and staged parties all over the country, and none, not even a presidential inaugural ball, even approaches the Bacchus rendezvous."

As the 1974 celebration concluded, consideration was already being given to Glen's successor. Because Bacchus kings are nationally recognized

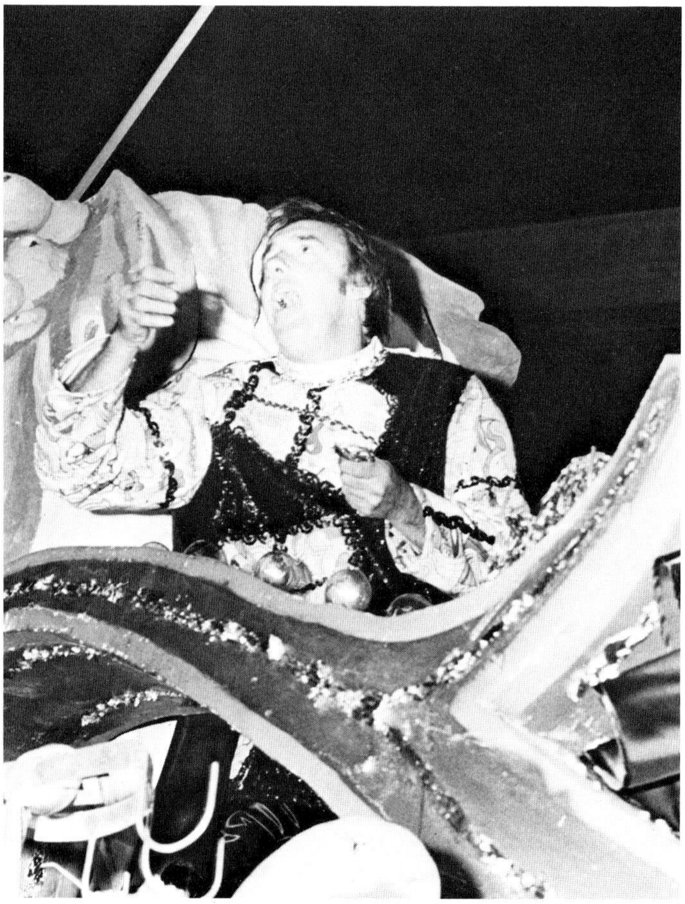

Nabors rides again.

Sometimes it rains doubloons.

Gawlee, Glen, I told you it would be fun.

celebrities, they hesitate to commit themselves too far in advance; who knows when a lucrative contract may be in the offing?

While approaches are made as far as a year in advance, the king is usually not invited formally until late fall, and his acceptance on a no-cancellation basis generally takes place in December, just a couple of months before Carnival.

No matter who Bacchus VII would be, Campbell had carried off his reign with pomp, circumstance, and a little down-home flair. A national folk music hero had given to Bacchus a spirit to which it has become accustomed.

This was the god, who upon hearing Blaine Kern complain about his chapped lips, whipped out his chapstick and offered it to the owner of the wind-ravaged kisser.

Aristocratic? Never.

Considerate and eager to help? The epitome of both.

For Glen, the experience of being god would imprint itself vividly on the backroads of his memory and forever be gentle on his mind.

EPILOGUE

Purposely shying away from developing into a treatise on the merits and demerits of Carnival, this volume has sought solely to examine an unusual phenomenon—the unbelievably rapid assent to influence, prominence, and acceptance of a new krewe in a city layered with strata upon strata of tradition-fattened sacred cows.

Few would deny that Bacchus has made it and made it big in six short years. Its objective to give "the people"—local citizenry, visitors, and traditionally excluded ethnic groups—wider participation, has been accomplished. And the historic aristocratic structure is solidly intact.

Nationwide recognition of Bacchus and the consequential fallout accruing to the benefit of Carnival, Mardi Gras, New Orleans, and Louisiana have exceeded the organization's fondest expectations. Each king has been a celebrity of national repute who reigned with majesty if not power.

There are still a few detractors. Some even try to read success as failure; *i.e.*, as overpowering as was Bob Hope's reign, timeless apostles of doom fretted about its effects. Had Bacchus reached its pinnacle of influence in five years only to be relegated henceforth to the downhill slopes? A narrow overview indeed.

True, Hope was the zenith of show biz. However, rather than a deadend in the road, Bacchus V opened up avenues of rapprochement with other celebrity-kingdom heavies who like to be numbered among colleagues at the top.

How many would quibble with a John "Bacchus" Wayne? A Bing "Bacchus" Crosby? A Paul "Bacchus" Newman? Johnny "Bacchus" Carson? Jackie "Bacchus" Gleason? How sweet it is—to contemplate these and other possibilities. Because of Hope it will be easier to attract people of that calibre.

Don't expect the infant krewe to rest on its grapes. Look for continuing innovations—super floats dwarfing the krewe's already larger ones, more animation, special doubloon issues, an annual network television special, super Superdome rendezvous! Some even contemplate a female king? Joy! Great joy, to the movement!

In a passage from "Fiddler on the Roof," Tevye's daughter, Hodel, is reminding her pretendu, Perchik, of the age-old custom decreeing that a boy show respect to a girl . . . realizing all the while that her people's traditions are old hat to an avant-garde chap like Perchik. When the young man mocks her customs, Hodel retorts with tempered conviction that her people are perfectly happy with their old ways. Perchik proceeds to bemoan selfishly the fact that customs are changing everywhere except in Hodel's village, where boys and girls can hardly look at one another let alone touch each other. The sheltered girl points out somewhat defensively that she is at the very moment looking at Perchik.

In the city, he says, young people are showing their affections without the assistance of a matchmaker. They're even holding hands and dancing together. At this juncture, he grabs Hodel and begins to dance. When Perchik asks if she likes it, Hodel underplays her apparent enthusiasm by calling it "nice." At which time, Perchik proudly pronounces a monumental change in customs. With that one act, a simple dance, tradition has been broken.

Like Hodel and Perchik, Bacchus has confirmed one expectation—once you make up your mind to change, or bend, or stretch tradition, the actual feat is not that difficult. It is the apprehension leading up to the coup itself that is painful.

"There, we've done it," Bacchus can say, knowing full well today's change will likely be tomorrow's tradition for the young but well entrenched krewe. Antithesis? Perhaps. But not the least bit perplexing when you live in the very real world of make-believe that is known as Carnival.